Pursue Your Purpose, Not Your Dreams
It Starts with You

by
Joe Johnson

Pursue Your Purpose, Not Your Dreams:
It starts with you!

Copyright © 2014 by Joe Johnson

Printed in the United States of America

First Printing, 2014

ISBN 978-0-9906092-0-9

This book is dedicated to all of the people in this world who continue to search for their purpose and for the people who are getting ready to find their true identity. I also want to dedicate this book to all of Milwaukee, WI, Milwaukee Public Schools, and my entire family for helping me become the person I am today. Lastly, this book is dedicated to "LIFE." Without "LIFE" I would not have experienced everything I have been through and without those experiences, I would have continued to be something/somebody I was not. Experiences changed me for the better!

Forward

Proud! This is the word that comes to mind when anticipating the impact of "Pursue your Purpose, Not your Dreams," on the lives of youth and young adults across the country. Pride is also the word that comes to mind when I consider all that my husband, partner, friend, confidant, and companion has extended to this book. Initially, I felt overwhelmed with the request to write the forward for this book. I questioned any bias I might have or if I was the "qualified" individual to make such an essential contribution and it dawned on me that I am the perfect person. I have witnessed my husband's desire to contribute to the lives of young people manifest itself in the text of this book. The vulnerability to use himself as a model for self assessment, inspiration, and challenge is truly admirable and needed. As a Psychologist who has spent years in K-12 and higher education, I recognize that many of us are well intentioned and even have genuine passion to help, mentor, and support. However, many of us are stuck in the world of academia and find it difficult to make sense of the world unless explained by statistics and the latest research.

I consider, "Pursue your Purpose, Not your Dreams," a masterpiece. A masterpiece because it appeals to the humanity of young men and women who may have lost their way or haven't considered all that he/she has to offer the world. This text was written in a way that will invite young people to read, learn, and remain open to assess themselves. This book was written in a way that will engage young people and hold their hand as they take action. You will find the words in the pages of this book to be honest, informative, and most distinctly - relatable. He has the capacity to reach lost souls or those of us that may be in conflict about how we desire to live our lives. The author, speaker and mentor, Joe Johnson has the skill to successfully meet readers right where they are. He will encourage, inspire, challenge, and invite readers to reflect on past successes and struggles, and at moments offer a swift kick in the ass in support of you stepping your game up.

Our world is plagued with limited self-esteem, self doubt, lack of skill development, and less than adequate mentorship. What is most disheartening is the cost of our societal limitations. We are full of astounding potential and promise that is rarely nurtured. Not only will "Pursue your Purpose, Not your Dreams" offer you access into the life of author Joe Johnson and allow you to assess his own personal struggles, it will also illustrate the ways he began to transform his thinking and behavior and extend tools to help you begin to do this for yourself. I extend a shared challenge - fully engage, buckle up, and prepare for transformation. Create the same honesty within yourself that author Joe Johnson demonstrates throughout the heartfelt recollections of his struggles AND do something about it! Discover and pursue your purpose.

In salute of your journey,
Dr. Brandi Pritchett-Johnson
Licensed Psychologist
Founder/CEO of Future 4 Teens

Table of Contents

Introduction

"Sometimes we see more with our eyes and mouth shut!"
- Unknown

As a child I always dreamed of playing professional basketball or football. I always thought the millions of dollars I would earn as a professional athlete would cure anything. What I failed to realize, is that there was so much more to me and I never knew how all the other parts of who I was would provide opportunities for my future. I could make people laugh, I was told I was handsome, people gravitated to me, I was very thoughtful of others, and I loved helping anyone. However, my focus was only on what I could do with my athletic ability.

It was very interesting because my mother and father always stressed education but my focus was far from academics. My mother did not graduate high school but she is one of the smartest people I know and my father ended up earning a college degree when he was older. Even though my parents were divorced, I received nothing but love and both wanted me to go to college.

Often there are stereotypes about single mothers without a high school degree raising their children. One stereotype is that they don't expect their children to go to college. Well, that was totally opposite for me because my mother stressed college all the time. My father did the same but for some reason like most children; I did do not like to listen to my parents. I did not understand the benefits of education, so I always resorted back to who I was as an athlete.

Through high school, I struggled academically. I ended up attending a community college on an athletic scholarship because my grade point average was low and my ACT score was not high enough to attend a university.

When I arrived at college, I realized college allowed me and other young adults opportunities to find out what we enjoyed in life, test our ability to handle adversity, and learn how to function in places that were different from where we grew up. I learned the struggles of dealing with people who would tell me no, I learned how to fail and pick myself up, and I also learned how to ask for help. Without experiencing college, I don't know how I would have gained some of the skills I have adapted to my everyday life.

Although I learned valuable lessons about life while in college and managed to have a good college football career, when it was time for me to graduate, the National Football League (NFL) was right at my fingertips. After training and working out for several teams, I received the devastating news that I would not get an opportunity to play in the NFL. Receiving this news turned my world upside down.

What happens to us when we think we've worked our whole life to do something and then the door is shut in our face? During this time, I felt like a failure and had no clue how my future would look.

I was lost because I would sit in my apartment and hear about other teammates getting opportunities in the NFL. I was excited for my college teammates getting picked up by the NFL but I was hurt because I never received a call.

As much as it hurt, the strength of my family and friends kept me strong. I needed to come up with a plan, so I did. I thought about everything I had done in my life and started to write down what brought me the most joy. By the end of my writing session, I realized how much I loved working with youth. That day was the beginning of my personal transformation.

This transformation made me tap into my natural skills of networking but I also humbled myself enough to ask for help. I realized during any transition period, it is vital to our success that we ask for help and seek out mentors or someone who has been where we are trying to go. Through networking and asking for help two men by the name of Dr. Lonnie Duncan and Dr. Joseph Morris helped me with the process of entering graduate school. They both saw potential in me and I ended up being accepted to graduate school.

After being accepted and focusing on my academics, three years later I received my master's degree and a school counselor license. What was more gratifying, were the opportunities I received during this time, the development of my own identity, and finding my purpose. I was able to learn from a couple of excellent faculty members, travel to professional conferences, meet prominent people in the counseling profession, work with community members, establish programs for youth in the community, and gain a new respect for education. Studying the counseling profession helped me look deep within and change the way I viewed the world but more importantly myself.

I learned to respect everyone's different experiences and views on life but I started to notice the amount of youth and adults who were throwing away potential because of identity issues and not understanding their purpose. The counseling profession also introduced me to reflection. I began to take time to reflect on my life and I started to see more clearly. I would ask my friends and the students I worked with, how often they reflected on life and I realized many of them never took time to reflect.

My reflections helped me realize the amount of ideas I would think of but I never took the time to make them a reality. I had ideas about books to write, businesses to open, programs to implement with youth, and speaking topics. Reflection was the jump-start to a new way of living for me and I believe it can do the same for others.

It is a necessity for us to sit and reflect on our lives. Think about it! We will take time for everything else and talk about the latest gossip, television shows, music videos, or sports games. But too often we do not reflect on what can create clarity in our lives. These two important areas are, "Who we are (Identity) and why we are here (Purpose)." Have we become so consumed with everything around us that we forget about ourselves? Or maybe there is so much going on in our lives that taking time to reflect seems like a hard task. The way I reflect is to find a quiet place by myself, close my eyes and begin to reflect on my childhood, people in my life, decisions I have made, goals I set, work I have done, and anything that comes to mind that affects my life.

So many of us are living day to day and have consumed ourselves in jobs or careers we hate but because we get a direct deposit check every two weeks, the comfort of knowing we have income coming in makes us stay put. We let people treat us like we are less than a person for the sake of fitting in. We hang around our so called "friends" but in reality they do not treat us with love or do anything real friends are supposed to. We also enable others around us and mistake it for helping. There is so much more we do to add to the stress in our lives and others but because we do not take a minute to reflect, we never learn who we really are (Identity) or why we are here (Purpose).

Take a minute to ask yourself, "When was the last time I reflected on my life?" If you reflect all the time, continue to do so. If you never reflect, close your eyes and take 30 seconds in total silence and reflect on your life and what you have read so far. Focus on whatever thoughts and feelings come to mind. When you open your eyes ask yourself, "How can I have the life I have always wanted? How can I find my purpose and live happily ever after? Why not me? What legacy do I want to leave for my children and grandchildren? Who am I really and how can I live according to the real me?" So, I am asking you to ask yourself, "Why not me?" and say to yourself, "It can be me!"

Get ready to begin the process of transforming the way you think, find out who you are (Identity), and why you are here (Purpose). LET'S START TODAY!

Your Pursuit of Purpose Starts with Understanding Yourself!

Activity #1
What Have I Done & What Brings Me Joy?

Take three minutes and write down all of the jobs you've had, all of the volunteering you've done, any time you've done some work for free, anything that you can think of.

Next, look at what you've written and think about what brought you the most joy. Ask yourself:

- What did I absolutely love doing?

- Why did it bring me so much joy?

- Could I do it for free?

- Was I good at what I was doing?

- Did others think I was good at what I was doing?

- What do I think it is that makes me enjoy it?

Notes

Chapter 1
Purpose vs. Dreams:
What do you mean?

"Sometimes your purpose finds you when
you least expect it."
-Unknown

Every living being comes from somewhere. However you define "somewhere," just like a track star, we have a start and we have a finish. What is more interesting is that we have many different starts and finishes in our lives. Therefore, just like the track star, we run many different races. Some people take off from the start fast like a sprinter and miss out on everything life has to offer and they forget about themselves. Others take off from the start like a long distance runner, nice and steady. They have time and energy to speed up when life is moving fast and they can slow down when life needs them to take a look at what's going on around them.

Dreams are the perfect example of how sprinting through life could cause us to miss out on what is meant for us. Purpose represents that long distance runner, moving through life nice and steady, with time to figure out the reason we are here. A lot of us seem to get our Purpose and our Dreams mixed up because we always thought they were the same. I know I did until I had that moment in life where I was "MENTALLY DECAPITATED" by an experience that caused me to look within myself and make distinctions between my Dreams and my Purpose.

Mental decapitation is when you have a major experience that makes you change the way you think about something. I will never forget the day my old mentality was chopped off and replaced with a new way of thinking. I told you about it earlier. You know, when not one NFL team called me. I always dreamed of playing in the NFL and I thought I was destined to be an NFL running back but I guess life had other plans.

Dreams

Dreams are okay to have as long as you are not sprinting through life. However, because so many of us are sprinting through life, not paying attention to what's going on inside ourselves or in our environment, we become focused on something that is not meant to be and we don't have a full understanding of what dreams are meant to do for us. For example, ask someone around you or ask yourself to define "Dream." I would bet that maybe one or two out of ten people would be able to define it. We would probably hear the usual, "Dreams are something that we have wanted for a long time" or "Dreams are fantasies that come true sometimes." I guess these definitions can be okay at a surface level but what about the definitions that have some depth and make us think deeply about what we believe our "Dreams" are? What we probably never realized is that when we uncover the surface layers of the word "Dream," we will read something different. *Dreams are a series of thoughts, images, or emotions during sleep. Dreams are ideas or visions that are created with your imagination and are not real.*

When I first looked up the definitions, I began to rethink my personal dreams I had during my life. I questioned whether or not my dream of playing in the NFL was real or just a fantasy. I always wonder how many people are misled by their dreams. We all know someone who has dreams of becoming a famous music artist or actor. We all know someone who dreams of being the next technology wiz. We all can look in the mirror and look at someone who has possibly been chasing a dream that could just be an idea or vision created with our imagination and is not real. Who knows! Many of us don't know because we are sprinting just like that track star and we miss the signs that tell us to slow down, go left, back up, jump, or start over. These signs may be spending too much money and or time without any benefits, no progress being made in whatever we are attempting to do, not recognizing our strengths (skills we have), and many others.

Are you sprinting toward your dream so fast that you get to the finish line and you're not happy with the outcome? It happens all the time. People have dreamed of living a certain lifestyle and plan their entire lives out in a week. They sprint toward a career in a certain area and they might make the money they dreamed of having, but they hate waking up to go to work. They hate the long hours, the stress, and they wake up one day with all the money in the world but their happiness has been jeopardized by this dream that caused them to sprint toward the life and career they "thought" they wanted. Now they look back with regrets on how much they missed out on because they were chasing a dream that was probably just an idea or vision leading them in the opposite direction of their purpose.

Dreams are okay and have a place in our lives but it's what we do with those dreams that determine the outcome at our finish line. When our life consists of sprinting, our dreams may cause us to end up in an area that is not meant for us. Think about what you call your dreams and ask yourself, "What do my dreams truly mean?"

Purpose

Purpose is the reason in which you exist. Purpose is something that everyone does not take into consideration. I would consider purpose as the single ingredient that brings us a sense of happiness. We know what they say, "When you find your purpose, you never work a day in your life." This is so true! However, the hard part for most of us is finding our purpose. Sometimes what we think is our purpose, ends up being that dream we had for years or a misinterpretation of who we are and why we are here.

Let's take it back to the long distance track star that starts off nice and steady. There is something about a steady pace that allows us to run for a long period of time. We have the ability to observe our environment, we have time to reflect on how we're moving, we have the strength to speed up and slow down when necessary, and we also have time to figure out our next move. This is very different than the sprinter who takes off and they're at the finish line before they know it.

Purpose takes time. It's not that purpose is something that we create, but it's something that is already meant for us, inside of us; and our job is to find it, understand it, and nurture it into something that benefits ourselves and others. For example, after I did not make it to the NFL, I needed to figure out my next move. Through reflection, I learned I have always loved working with youth and for some reason every job I liked was dealing with young people. I found my purpose by paying attention to the themes of my life that made me the happiest. Even when I tried to work in corporate America, I realized the money could potentially be great but I would not be happy because my purpose was not in corporate America or chasing money. My purpose was working with our youth.

Remember, we don't create our purpose, we find our purpose or our purpose finds us. So even when we run away from what we are meant to do, purpose finds its way back into our lives. Some people fight purpose and have the ability to endure the pain of living outside their purpose. We see it happening all the time with teachers or professors. The teacher or professor knows and their students know that teaching is not their purpose because their teaching styles have never connected with their students. However, because they have spent years getting a degree in an area to teach, they stick with it. This is devastating to the teachers and professors lives and the lives of the students they're teaching because the students are not learning.

When we are not living our purpose, it's emotionally draining. People can see our pain, our style is not very effective, the language we use toward people is not always positive, and then we burnout because we are unhappy.

We find our purpose by staying true to our values. Our values are the things we believe are important in the way we live. They probably determine our priorities and they are ingrained in our mind, body, and soul. What is also interesting about our values is that they can change during our lives and that is perfectly fine. However, no matter how much our values change, I can guarantee they will align with our purpose which never changes.

Examples of Values

Loyalty	Trust
Open Minded People	Family
Honesty	Respecting others beliefs
Accountability	Happiness
Friendship	Exploration
Education	Money
Helping Others	Power
Laughter	Unity

You are probably asking yourself, "What do I value?" and "Can we have more than one purpose?" It's important for us to know what we value and live by them because our values will be challenged throughout life and when we dishonor our values, we move further away from our purpose.

Our purpose is already here and our job is to find it or except it when our purpose finds us. I cannot tell you how many purposes we have but I will say, purpose is not something that is scattered. For example, my purpose is working with youth and I do that by speaking to different youth around the country, running a youth organization, worked as a school counselor, and mentor as many of our youth as possible. My purpose is in the area of working with youth and I do that in multiple ways. This is different than saying, my purpose is to work with youth and my other purpose is to be a police officer. That's two different areas and purpose does not work that way.

It's important for us to understand that life is a journey and this includes the journey of finding our purpose. Through our experiences in life, we will find out what we love and who we are as a person. We will learn everyone goes through times where they thought they loved something and were close to finding their purpose, but in reality it was just another stepping stone to finding purpose. The wisdom we gain through this journey, keeping that nice and steady pace like the long distance track star, will allow us to come to an understanding with ourselves about our purpose. When we get to this point, we must understand our purpose, nurture it and continue to live in it because some people never find purpose and when they almost get to the finish line, they ask themselves, "How did I get here?"

Purpose vs. Dreams

We live in a time where everyone wants immediate gratification or results. I will be the first one to tell you, just like the sprinter who takes off fast and misses everything (Dream), our Purpose does not always happen on our time table according to how fast we want it. Trust the process of learning yourself just like the long distance track star who keeps the nice and steady pace. Stay true to your values and pay close attention to how situations make you feel because if we're chasing what we think is our purpose and it's pulling us away from our values and we feel something is not right, it's probably just a dream. For example, if I valued "honesty" and what I thought was my purpose forced me to lie to others in order for me to make lots of money, it's probably just a dream. If we've spent time and money on what we think is our purpose and we seem to always run into a dead end, it's probably just a dream. When our thoughts and actions have nothing to do with one another and the people around us see something different than what we see in ourselves, we should always reflect and ask ourselves if we're living a dream or our purpose. When our mind, body and soul, tells us to go in one direction but we feel the need to do something different because of the voice of others, we should double check and ask ourselves, "Is this my purpose?"

We have all been molded by our family, friends, experiences, and other things in our life. It's okay to let our dreams flow because sometimes they guide us to our purpose. However, do not get sucked into pursuing a dream that takes you away from the reason you are alive. Your Purpose!

Notes

CHAPTER 2
What is your Cool?
"Learn, Unlearn, Re-Learn"
- Dr. Calvin Mackie

Growing up as a child it seemed like I was convinced by my family and the world that being a doctor (medical doctor) or a lawyer was the way to go. I remember hearing other children say the same about what they wanted to be when they grew up but I also heard children talk about being a police officer, a fire fighter, a professional athlete or a movie star. Was I really interested in these professions and did other children just so happen to have the same interest? Or maybe, society and the world around us thought it would be great for me and other children to become interested in certain professions that were considered to be "Cool." These professions were probably considered "Cool" for some but looking back, I don't think many of the professions would have been interesting to me if it were not for the influence of society, family and friends.

So, what is "Cool"? Where does "Cool" come

from? How can I become "Cool"? These are probably questions we all have internally with ourselves. It's not like we walk around asking people or taking notes on what it means to be "Cool," but we often want to be seen as a person who is "Cool."

Here are a few areas we may think about that are connected with being "Cool":

Our Hair	Our Skin	Our Teeth	Our Eyebrows	Our Fingernails
Clothes We Wear	The Car We Drive	House	Career	Job
How we walk	Shoes	Our Friends	Boyfriend	Girlfriend
Husband	Wife	Our Faith/ Religion	Family	School
How we talk	Personalities	Perceived Image	Education	Neighbor-hoods
Street Credibility	Sex Life	Body Image	Hygiene	Sexuality
Mental Stability	Image	Potential	Finances	How we make $$$

As I grew older (middle school and high school), "Cool" for me became the ability to walk into a room without saying a word and everyone noticed me. Being "Cool" was the ability, as a man, to have multiple women in my life, become a standout athlete, have some money in my pocket, keep a clean haircut and have good looks. For a woman, I thought they had to have a nice body, beautiful face, and a sweet attitude. Finally, having the ability to befriend anyone and everyone multiplied my coolness because of the relationships I could establish. This is what I thought made the ultimate "Cool" individual.

These thoughts came from society and the portrayal of males and females, my neighborhood, but most of all, my beliefs came from listening and watching older friends and family every day.

I will never forget the first time I spoke to a girl on the phone. I used every line I heard my older cousin use and after about four lines, I did not have anything else to say. I even tried to use the same tone of voice and mimic the body language he used when talking to girls on the phone. This same cousin also sold drugs to get money and I thought he was so "Cool" because he had women, money, and he dressed nice.

These personal experiences are a little ridiculous and funny but the realities of life are that many of us fall victim to the influence of others and societal factors that cause us to make decisions based on other's perceptions of what is "Cool." We buy certain clothing lines because we see television stars or already deemed "Cool" people wearing the clothes. The cars we buy are based on what is "Cool" at the time instead of what we can actually afford. The type of language we use when having conversations are based off the hottest new "Cool" slang words. The people we date are often based on the outside appearances of men or women because many think, "If you look cool, then you must be cool."

I have worked with many K-12 and college students and many of them would come to school every day and not do any work in the classroom. However, they would love to talk about how nerdy other students were who did their work. They would even have friends who were great students but they, themselves, continued to do poorly in school. I never understood why students would come to school to do nothing. Then I thought about it, even I had a mild case of this situation because being smart has never really been considered "Cool" above being athletic, having money, having nice clothes, or having the best looking girlfriend or boyfriend. I have even met people who are unemployed tell me, "I'm looking for a job but I will not work at a fast food place because it's not a good look for me." So I guess being broke is a good look for them! Wrong! Some of us would rather have no money than to work at a fast food restaurant because for many, working at a fast food restaurant is not "Cool"!

It is important for us to understand where we are in our life and think about some of the things we consider to be "Cool." Is something "Cool" because we have a genuine liking for it or have we been conditioned by society, family, and friends to believe something is "Cool" for false reasons.

I will never forget my experience with my "Cool" reality check. I went to see a speaker by the name of Dr. Calvin Mackie. I had no clue who this guy was but I've always loved to hear different motivational speakers whenever I had the opportunity to see them in person.

The event was held in a pretty big auditorium and for some reason only about 30 people showed up. I thought about leaving but when he started to speak, I was very intrigued by his message and his life story. I remember a few of his mini messages during his time speaking but I will never forget Dr. Mackie telling us, "...we need to have the ability to LEARN, UNLEARN, and RE-LEARN!" When he said this, I had a chill feeling go through my body because it hit home.

We have been taught by society, family and friends what is "Cool." We have all made decisions based on false beliefs about school, careers, relationships, finances, and many more. Some of us have missed out on opportunities because we did not think it was "Cool" enough for us. We have treated people wrong because they did not fit our perceived image of what "Cool" is. We've done so much damage to ourselves because we never took the time to ask ourselves, "What is 'Cool' for me, myself, and I?"

So many of us have a hard time finding

ourselves in a society that is filled with false images of what it means to be "Cool." Re -evaluate your world and yourself and re-define your definition of "Cool" and as you read the rest of this book, remember the three words I continue to live by, "Learn, Unlearn, and Re-Learn."

Activity #2
What is cool to you?

Write down your top 5 things that are cool to you.

1.

2.

3.

4.

5.

Next, ask yourself what makes them so cool? (Is it because you believed it or were you influenced?)

1.

2.

3.

4.

5.

Notes

CHAPTER 3

The Negative Things in Your Life!

"You can't live a positive life with a negative mind."

- Unknown

Who Cares!

Do not waste your time focusing on the negative!

CHAPTER 4
Positive Thinking

"He who says he can and he who says he can't, are both usually right."
–Confucius

Throughout our entire lives, we will all go through stress, unforeseen situations, the feelings of failure, and times where it seems like nothing is going your way. It could be related to work, school, issues with family and friends, physical or mental health issues, and most of all it could be an internal battle with "self." Everyone does not make it through these situations. However, I believe everyone has the capability of making it through. Recognizing the first step of getting through any rough time in your life involves a personal commitment to positive thinking!

I remember having conversations with one of my students about everything going on in their life. The student was struggling with family dysfunction, money issues, and everything else that negatively affected his focus in school. As I sat and listened, I could not help but notice the student's attitude toward everything negative happening all at once. Naturally when we go through something positive or negative, we have emotions that we use to express how we feel and this is okay. However, our emotions have the ability to paralyze our rational thinking. Meaning, the way we react and navigate fixing whatever situation we are going through could be jeopardized. Included is our ability to think positive about getting through tough situations.

As I moved forward with my student, I brought up my thoughts on the way the student seemed to be thinking negatively about everything. I would have been okay if the student had a few negative thoughts for a couple days but when these thoughts continued for a few weeks, I had to address the way I perceived the student was thinking. I told the student about some of the phrases used during our conversations that led me to become worried about their capacity to handle these life situations. Some of the phrases were the same phrases many of us have used at some point when we have dealt with our own situations. Phrases like, "Nothing is going right in my life," "I hate my life," "I don't care anymore," "I want to kill myself," "I wish I was not born," "This will never get better," and many others. Sometimes people might not use these phrases verbally, but they're thinking the same thing. Either way, whether these phrases are said verbally or thought about, they can affect our ability to get past situations in our life that we don't want.

It is also important for us to recognize when we begin to have thoughts like these because there are so many people who deal with "Depression." Depression is sometimes described as feeling sad, unhappy, miserable, or down. Some of us have short periods where we feel this way but others can sometimes have a severe case of depression and these symptoms last for a long time. Either way, recognizing and acknowledging these feelings should alarm you to seek help. Just like the time I didn't get picked up by an NFL team, I needed help and we all need some type of help when we go through tough times.

The student and I began to work on his skills to think positive. As his skills grew, his thinking slowly changed for the better. His attitude started to change, the language he used started to change, he smiled more, and although some of the same situations continued in his life, they were not affecting his ability to live as much as before because of his new way of thinking.

I believe one of the best ways to live our lives is to always remember that waking up in the morning is not promised and every time we wake up, we should consider it a positive moment in our lives. When we have the opportunity to live and pursue our purpose, we cannot forget about how important the "little things" are in life. I assume that often we consider the "little things" in life nothing more than something that is supposed to happen. The air we breathe, our health, the food we have access to, the clothes we wear, the roof over our heads, and so many others. We become so focused on the negative in our lives that we forget some people have no food, people use machines to help them breathe, people are homeless, and a lot of people in this world barely have clothes to put on their backs. I have been fortunate enough to meet several people who are living in situations where they have nothing but their outlook on life makes them seem like they have it all. When we don't think positive and focus on the negative in our lives, we forget how fortunate we are to just wake up in the morning.

Many of us are at home wondering why our family is so dysfunctional, at our job wondering "Why am I here?", at school struggling to make it to graduation, and some of us are having this internal fight with ourselves because we feel lost and have not found our purpose in life. When we realize we're not alone because there are millions of people who are going through the same situations, it is sometimes easier to begin to think positive. I have been there myself and one way to begin to dig ourselves out of a hole that feels too deep to get out of, is to start with ourselves and think positive.

The way we think will control the way we live and the way we live will sometimes control how long we live. Our thoughts often become our realities and I hope we all want positive realities. Thinking positive is easier said than done. Being committed to this new way of thinking and the way you view your life situations, is vital. I would be lying to you if I said I don't have negative thoughts. However, all of my positive thoughts outweigh my negative thoughts and for every one negative thought, I have hundreds of positive thoughts that help to get me through my tough times and I know it can do the same for you!

Activity #3
The Positive Thinking Starter Kit:
Ask Yourself...

Did I wake up this morning? . . . . . . Yes No

Do I have 10 fingers and 10 toes? . . . Yes No

Do I have clothes to put on? . . . . . . Yes No

Do I have shoes to put on?. . . . . . . Yes No

Do I have the ability to walk on

  my own? . . . . Yes No

Do I have vision? . . . . Yes No

Do I have a place to live?. . . . . Yes No

Do I have family members to talk to?. Yes No

Do I have friends to talk to? . . . . . . Yes No

Do I have a sense of humor?. . . . . . Yes No

Do I care for others? . . . . Yes No

Do I smile often? . . . . Yes No

Do I have the ability to read? . . . . . Yes No

Do I have a job/career? . . . . Yes No

Do I have the ability to find a

  job/career?. . . . . Yes No

Do I have the mental capability

  to function? . . . . Yes No

Do I have food to eat every day? . . . Yes No

Do I have the ability to be creative?. . Yes No

Other:_____ . . Yes No

Other:_____ . . Yes No

Other:_____ . . Yes No

Who are you?

I am nice to others . . . . Yes No

I love myself. . . . . Yes No

I love my family . . . . Yes No

I love my friends . . . . Yes No

I like the simple things in life. . . . . . Yes No

I breathe on my own . . . . Yes No

I always give my best effort . . . . . . Yes No

I know what I am good at . . . . Yes No

I have a unique skill that no
   one knows about . . . . Yes No

I am responsible . . . . Yes No

People count on me . . . . Yes No

I am a role model. . . . . Yes No

I have a great imagination . . . . Yes No

I am a problem solver . . . . Yes No

I am a fast learner . . . . Yes No

I have a passion for something . . . . Yes No

I know what I have a passion for . . . Yes No

What situations in your life do you want to change?

What are some of the thoughts you have had with yourself because of the situations you mentioned?

What are some ways to think positively about the situation(s)?

What are some positive thoughts about yourself?

What steps will you take to begin the process of thinking positive?

Notes

CHAPTER 5
Facing the Realities of Life

"The reality is, at some point we all must face reality."

-Unknown

For so long I would hear my family and friends say to me and others, "Keep it real" or "Keep it 100." This statement was made when somebody wanted the truth, the whole truth, and nothing but the truth! So, I have to "Keep it 100" because nobody should want to deal with the whole problem with half the truth.

Earlier in chapter three I said we should not focus on the negative things in life and we shouldn't. However, because I want to "Keep it real" and be completely truthful, I have to bring awareness to and acknowledge some of the realities of life that we all may go through from time to time. I want to make sure we understand and can recognize situations in life that could have negative effects on our ability to maximize our potential headed toward our purpose.

Worrying About Everyone Else

The first is worrying about everyone else except the person we see in the mirror every single day of our lives. We all have made the statement, "Don't worry about me, worry about yourself." This is very interesting because a lot of us making this statement are doing exactly the opposite of what we are telling others to do. I am pretty sure you are reading this statement and wondering two things. One, "Do I make this statement?", and two, "Do I worry about everyone else?" The answer is, more than likely yes and yes. If you don't constantly worry about others, continue that habit.

Every time I think about people who constantly worry about others, I think about two different types of worrying. I also think about one of my aunts who would always worry about my cousin's and I when we were younger.

My cousins and I would get so mad at this particular aunt because she would always run to our grandmother and tell her everything we were doing that was bad. Why did she worry about us? Shouldn't she mind her own damn business as an adult and worry about what she was doing? No! This type of worrying about others is okay and often necessary for people who need a little guidance. After all, we were kids and probably would have done even more wild things if my aunt did not tell my grandmother on us. We would have also missed out on much of the wisdom given to us by my grandmother while she reprimanded us.

The second type of worrying is when we are so focused on what our family, friends, or someone we may or may not know is doing, that we lose focus on what is going on in our own lives. We sometimes become jealous of what others have, we begin to point out all the flaws someone may have, we start to measure what's going on in our lives compared to everyone else's, and then we forget to do all the small things needed to continue on our personal path to our purpose. This will sometimes lead to questioning ourselves and our personal goals, loss of relationships with family and friends and finally, sometimes getting the reputation of what many would call a "Hater." I define a "Hater" as someone who always has something negative to say about someone or their accomplishments.

Worrying is probably a natural experience for all of us but understanding what type of worrying we are doing could be the difference between moving forward toward our purpose or moving backwards. To make it clear, "Worry about your own damn self and make sure you are doing what is necessary to move toward maximizing your potential headed toward your purpose."

The Pressure

Pressure is often defined as, "the action of a force against an opposing force," or "the stress or urgency of matters demanding attention," and finally, "the burden of physical or mental distress." For example, if we were to put our hands together in front of us like we were praying and try to push one hand away from the other, that would be "pressure" according to the first definition (Try it!). Next, if we are at work or school and we have four to five projects or assignments due around the same date and we feel "pressure" to get them done, that is an example of the second definition. Understanding the difference between these two types of pressure is important. However, I want to focus on the third definition of "pressure" and how it could affect our ability to discover our purpose.

The third definition of <u>pressure</u> states, "pressure is the burden of physical and mental distress." Meaning there could be situations in our lives that cause physical or mental distress. Distress is just something that causes pain or suffering to the body or mind. All of us have had some type of pressure that affected us physically or mentally. If you are reading this and saying to yourself, "Not me," check yourself because pressure comes in many ways and sometimes we do not recognize "pressure."

If you have played any type of sport, you understand the hours and hours of practice that must take place in order to make sure we perform at a high enough level to play in the game. If you grew up with brothers and sisters or any family members, sometimes there is a friendly level of competition that drives each person to want to be a little better than the other family member. If you ever had a job or had to go to school, there is a certain time that we must be there in order to not be considered late. Sometimes we do everything we can to make sure we are not late. Well some of us! But you get the point. All of these examples have a hint of "pressure" associated with them. Let me explain. But first, think about your own life and answer the questions below.

What types of "pressure(s)" are happening in your life right now?

1._____

2. _____

3._____

4._____

5._____

Pressure brings out the best in some of us and the worst in others. Imagine being jobless for six months and down to your last penny. You're finally asked to interview for a position that would provide you with enough income and satisfaction that all of your problems would seem to be wiped away. How do you react to the pressure of having an opportunity to turn your life around but knowing there is a possibility that you may not get the job and continue to be in a state of struggle?

Often, "pressure" seems to shift the mind into *one dimensional thinking*. In this case, we may only think about the negative outcomes and lose focus of our goal. In the example with the job interview, all our thoughts would be focused on not getting the position and what it would be like to struggle for another six months. Some people have been known to let the pressure get to them so much that they begin to doubt their abilities, become insecure, and their confidence level drains to zero. In the immediate moment of dealing with pressure, some people begin to sweat, lose their appetite, and even lose their ability to think clearly. All of this happens because sometimes pressure brings out the worst in us.

Just to be clear, many of us become anxious when dealing with pressure. Anxious is described by the *Merriam-Webster* dictionary as, "feeling afraid or nervous especially about what may happen." Mental health professionals may sometimes describe sweating, loss of appetite, and losing our ability to think clearly as symptoms of something called Anxiety or Anxiety Disorder. It's important to pay attention to what's happening to us during times of pressure. Physical symptoms such as losing or gaining weight rapidly, shaking, feeling weak, having a lack of energy, and many others can also be something to look for. Both emotional and physical reactions to pressure can be more extreme for some so pay close attention to how your body reacts.

However, we have the capacity to use "pressure" to bring out our competitive spirit. We begin to think about nothing but the positive outcomes of the situation. Yes, we acknowledge the possibility of something bad happening but our entire focus is on preparing ourselves to compete and perform at our highest level.

We visualize ourselves shaking hands after the interview and hearing the words, "You're hired." We would think about the level of peace we would have after struggling for six months. Most of all, our attitude and thought process in dealing with this "pressure" would have nothing but positive vibes, no matter what.

What is most important about pressure, is that it is just a test to see how we will react. We are all capable of conquering everything that comes with the pressures of life and it starts with mastering the way we think about whatever pressure situation we're dealing with. The more positive we allow ourselves to be, the easier it will be to deal with this so called monster we call "pressure."

Failure

Before I begin to talk about failure, let's make sure we are clear about what failure could be. Failure is defined as "the condition or fact of not achieving the desired end or ends." It can also be defined as "a lack of success."

Here's a list of several areas where we may feel a lack of success:

Homework Assign- ments	Test	Relation- ships	Sports	Jobs/ Careers
Parenting	Managing Money	Cooking	Weight loss	Public Speaking
Teaching	School	Marriage	Reestab- lishing Credit	Follow Through
Communi- cating	Goal Setting	Learning a Language	Network- ing	Marketing Yourself
Quitting an Addiction	Starting a Business	Entering the Enter- tainment Business	Following Dreams	Knowing Who You Are (Identity)

There is something about failure or failing that makes success that much sweeter. There is also something about failure or failing that causes many of us to lose the desire to chase success. What is it about failing that makes us view ourselves or the world differently? Why do we begin to use the word "can't" seconds, minutes, or hours after we have failed at something? If we are not careful, an incident of failing could be the start of an ongoing relationship with becoming comfortable with failure. This means many of us can become "best friends" with being okay about failing during our lives.

We have all failed many times in life. Bill Gates, the owner of Microsoft talks about the amount of times he failed tests in college. Michael Jordan, arguably the greatest professional basketball player even talks about being cut from the varsity basketball team in high school. Then there are countless music artist who often discuss the amount of times they were not given a record deal before their big break. Incidents of failure do not mean you will always be a failure in life.

I will never forget the struggles I had in high school, trying to go to college. Even though I was the football player of the year in my conference, I just finished playing in the state championship basketball game and I felt I was on top of the world, my high school grades were terrible. I finished high school with a 1.6 grade point average and my ACT (standardized test) score was only a 13 out of 36. I had several schools contacting me about playing football but my grades were not up to standards for four year universities. I ended up attending a community college in Arizona to play football and before I knew it I was cut from the football team before the season began.

This was one of my first major incidents where failure took everything out of me. I cried for a few hours, I laid in my bed for a full day, and I did not have energy to do anything. Just imagine being the best of the best your entire life and when you finally get to a point where you are feeling good about yourself and the abilities you have, you're told, "you're not that good."

Even though the coach did not tell me I was not that good, his action to cut me from the team expressed his views. This is what you can call an "implicit" way of communicating a message. An "explicit" way of communicating a message would have been the coach telling me verbally, "you are not that good." However, dealing with my first major incident with failure changed my attitude and the way I view failing.

I started to recognize the distress failure caused for many people. Too often when we fail, we begin to lose the confidence we have in ourselves. Even when we have the necessary skills and abilities to be great in a certain area, failing seems to drain our ability to think positively. Failing begins to change the language we use and begins to reshape the way we see the world we live in. For example, when the coach cut me from the team and I left his office, I started to think about what I did wrong in order for me to be in this situation. I started to feel like I could not be successful in college football but then I also remembered feeling like the world was an evil place and people would judge me based on failing.

When you are around people who feel like they have continuously failed, you begin to notice the language they use and the negative attitudes they have toward life in general. Words such as "can't" and "never" will often come out of their mouths. For example, when you share an idea with someone who has been affected by failure, they might tell you, "That will never happen" or "You can't do that." They may also begin to tell you how the world works from their point of view and talk about how you can only do certain things in life. This attitude and negative shift in language could happen to anyone when dealing with failure.

I learned to use failure as a tool to motivate myself internally. Instead of changing my attitude and thinking negatively about life, I began to find ways to strengthen areas that would help to make me successful in the future. This does not mean we become successful overnight but it means we are gradually working to do and be better than we were before.

In the case of playing college football, I worked out harder and smarter in the weight room, I made sure to study for my classes, and before I knew it I was playing football at a four year university and one of the best players in the nation. It was my mindset and my attitude toward the abilities I knew I always had that helped with my ability to overcome my incident of failure.

We should ask ourselves, "What type of person am I when failure enters my life?" Think about how you react to failure and what is it you would like to do differently. When you begin to recognize how your mind, body, soul, language, attitude, and feelings react to failure, you will be able to change for the better and turn failure into success.

Notes

CHAPTER 6
Check Yourself
"You better check yourself before
you wreck yourself."
-Ice Cube

How do we begin to set ourselves on a path to our purpose from the beginning or if we just finished dealing with problems in our lives? Simple, we need to wake up, focus, and then check ourselves! This is easier said than done, like many other "to do" sayings in life. However, this is where we begin to be honest with ourselves and learn to commit to self, maximizing our potential, and purpose.

Checking ourselves means recognizing the people we surround ourselves with and the bad habits we may have picked up from years of doing something the same way over and over again. Checking ourselves means changing the way we think and opening ourselves up to possibilities and opportunities we ruled out earlier in our lives. Checking ourselves means acknowledging our strengths and building on some of the skills we already have. Checking ourselves means giving up parts of our lives that have caused us to run away from success and our purpose (drugs, alcohol, sex, video games, friends, family, etc). Checking ourselves means waking up earlier and not sleeping our entire day away. Checking ourselves means being aware of how others perceive us (image). Checking ourselves means paying attention to our "personal brand." But most of all, checking ourselves begins with understanding who we are (identity) and why we are here on this earth (purpose).

Every journey to purpose begins somewhere. Most people believe the starting point is a physical place like at home or at school. Believe it or not, the journey to our purpose and success begins mentally, in our minds, the way we think, and what we believe about who we are.

There are so many people who have lived an unfulfilled life because of situations that caused them to miss out on opportunities. There are also people who allow others to create a pathway to destruction. We all know someone who has fallen into this situation. If we were to break down the core of the individual's issue, I would bet an identity issue and or a self-esteem issue would be at least part of the problem.

For example, there was a young teenage girl who was physically gorgeous. Her family was well known in the community and money was no issue. She always had a lot of friends and all of the other girls wanted to be like her. All of her life, she was told by her mother to use her beauty to get what she wanted. After leaving high school, she went off to college in another state where nobody knew about her family and she was the new girl in town. She was now surrounded by other individuals who looked good physically and using her beauty to get what she wanted did not work like it used to. This is when her world was turned upside down.

By the end of her freshman year of college, this young lady was pregnant and had a reputation of sleeping around with random men. She dropped out of college and ended up back home with her family that now treats her like trash because they believe she messed up the family reputation.

How can someone who seemed to have a wonderful life growing up, end up in a situation like this young lady? Let me tell you: identity, self-esteem and understanding purpose!

Identity can be defined in many ways but I define identity as, "distinct characteristics that belong to an individual based on values, beliefs, and experiences." For example, the young lady described in this chapter seemed to have her identity wrapped up in her physical characteristics (physical beauty). Therefore, anything and everything was consumed by her physical beauty. She was taught to use her physical beauty to function in life. Therefore, she valued the power related to her physical beauty.

Self-esteem can be defined in many ways as well. However, I define self-esteem as, "the confidence you have in yourself and the satisfaction about who you are." Her self-esteem seemed to be high throughout life when everyone knew her and her physical beauty benefited her. But when she got to college and there were people who cared less about her physical beauty, she started to lose the self-esteem she had and turned to doing something that she thought would benefit her (sleeping around). She ended up with a bad reputation, pregnant, and out of college.

The example illustrates one situation but there are many life examples of the loss of identity, self-esteem and purpose. How do you make it so that it's less likely you will be in a situation where your life is turned upside down because of loss of identity, self-esteem, and purpose? Let's check ourselves real quick!

We have to put this in perspective and understand there is no such thing as a simple quick fix. We all experience life or situations differently and we know that everyone does not have the same issues. So, let me speak on what I have noticed in my life and some of the experiences I've had with other people.

One of the best examples for me that explain identity, self-esteem, and purpose is my life as an athlete. I am sure other athletes have dealt or are dealing with the same issue on different levels. However, some athletes find a way to re-create themselves and some don't.

As I mentioned before, I was a gifted athlete and I played all kinds of sports. I would always play with the older kids and when I was in middle school, I started to play with grown men. Football and basketball were the two sports I fell in love with. Basketball was the number one sport for me because I could play every day and all my friends played. Looking back, I was probably better at football but I could still play with the best of the best in basketball.

In elementary school, I was better than everyone in the basketball league. In middle school, I was better than most in the basketball league and started to dominate in my football league. Then in high school, I became one of the best players at my high school, played in the state basketball championship game my senior year, and I was one of the best football players in the state. I say all this to paint a picture of what it means to be known for your athletic ability almost your entire life.

When you are known for your athletic ability as an athlete, you begin to believe in yourself and your self-esteem is high when you are playing those sports. You also begin to associate your identity with your athletic ability. For example, people would say, "Joe Johnson, who plays football and basketball," and you also get some athletes who say, "My name is _____, you know me, I play basketball." Instead of being Joe Johnson the person, I became Joe Johnson, "the athlete" to others and to myself.

As athletes we begin to place all of our identity into our ability to be great in the sport(s) we play. We have such high self-esteem in our athletic ability, people love us because of the sport(s) we play, and we begin to feel so good about ourselves that we forget about everything else that we are capable of doing and lose sight of our purpose. I was so consumed in playing sports in high school and college that I forgot about my abilities to learn academically. I always did just enough to keep my grade point average up so that I could play in the next game. This is what's called "situational self-esteem." You have high self-esteem in one area of life and low self-esteem in other areas of life.

Just like athletes, there are many people in the world who deal with "situational self-esteem" every day. I do not know a lot of people who have high self-esteem in everything they do. This example of athletes is just one example of the many ways in which we could lose our sense of identity, self-esteem, and purpose.

It is vital for us to think about where we are in our lives and ask ourselves, "Who am I?" (Identity) and "Why am I here?"(Purpose). Think about what we need in order to recognize our identity and build our self-esteem so that we can become successful staying on our path to our purpose. In other words, it's time to check ourselves!

Who Am I? (Identity)
Why Am I Here? (Purpose)

I am... (Who Am I?)

(You cannot say what you like to do or roles you have. For example, You cannot say, "I like basketball or I work at a shoe store." Use ADJECTIVES!) Adjectives are words used to describe something.

_____

_____

_____

_____

_____

_____

_____

What are your Values?

(Values are your "Personal Beliefs" that determine your priorities, choices, actions, thoughts, and what matters most to you.) For example, some people value Power, Money, Health, Friendship, etc.

_____

_____

_____

_____

_____

_____

_____

_____

What do you think is your PURPOSE as of today?

If you do not know, write down everything you have done in your life that makes you happy or you could do for "Free." For example, I always loved working with kids and would do it for free.

_____

_____

_____

_____

_____

_____

_____

_____

Notes

CHAPTER 7
Rebuilding You

"Rebuilding can begin at anytime. You do not need to begin the process when you are at Rock Bottom."

-Unknown

When I Google the word "rebuild" or "rebuilding," pictures and videos of people putting cars or buildings back together come up on the website. There was one video that displayed some guys putting a jeep back together in four minutes. There were also several pictures of entire cities or towns being rebuilt. I was hoping I would find pictures or videos of people rebuilding themselves because the rebuilding process of individuals take place often.

I believe everyone in the world goes through some type of rebuilding process at some point in their lives. One source defines the word rebuild as, "to repair, especially to dismantle and reassemble with new parts." When I read this definition I started to think about what happens during this process right after we have "checked ourselves"? Or maybe we are already in the rebuilding stage when we begin to check ourselves. What do you think?

I can remember several times in my life where I had to repair, dismantle, and reassemble with new parts. However, one of my greatest struggles in life was transitioning from being an athlete. I will never forget the day I checked myself and realized football would not be in my life anymore. As much as it hurt knowing the game I played almost all my life would be over, it hurt even more because I had no idea what I would do next. I had all kinds of thoughts in my head from hoping I would get a random call from an NFL team, winning the lottery, having a family with no job, and even selling drugs. Everything was running through my mind because of this fear of the unknown. When we are at a point in our lives where everything is changing, including us, it gets scary.

When we're rebuilding ourselves, sometimes we know how we want to turn out. However, sometimes we just know there needs to be some changes and we have no idea of the outcome.

I knew I had to repair some broken parts of me and reassemble them with new parts. If not,

I could have become one of those people who mentally beat themselves down because I did not accomplish what I thought was my purpose in life (football). At this point, the fear I had was real because my focus for years was only on my athletic ability. I forgot about all the other areas about myself that I never attempted to explore. Especially my ability to succeed in academics and using my mind to be successful.

Too often we forget about our potential. We forget about our ability to learn new things. We forget about our ability to work smarter not harder. We forget about our ability to rebuild ourselves when needed.

In my rebuilding process, the fear was real because I was making conscious decisions to focus on areas of my life that I did not see or shall I say, I did not care to see. I had no clue who I would be or where I would go when I started to focus on using my mind instead of my athletic ability.

Fear often stops us during the rebuilding process because we all would like to know what's in store for us in the future but we can't.

Fear often makes us believe that the "something different for me" is not available. Fear also creates a mentality of, "going back to what we are used to."

I say FEAR is, "Forget Everything And Run." This means, fear makes us run in the opposite direction of where we should be going (Our Purpose) and consumes us so much that we forget everything we already know about our potential and rebuilding ourselves. I also say FEAR is, "Finding Excuses About Reality." Too many times we know at some point we need to do certain things and we avoid them due to fear. In college, I would not take this mandatory class because I was scared I would fail. I was told over and over that the class was hard. Semester after semester, I had every excuse not to take it but in reality I needed to take the class at some point to graduate. Fear makes us come up with every excuse not to do something even when we know it has to happen.

Fear stopped me before but I was always the type of person who would at least put up a fight. When fear came knocking during this rebuilding process, I stood toe to toe and was so focused on creating a new me that after I pushed passed this case of fear, I began to see more of the potential I had and my purpose was starting to become clearer. I started to realize some of the strengths I've always had but never nurtured. I also opened up my scope of life by exposing myself to different groups of people, information, and opportunities. For example, when I was in Michigan I met a group of students from Saudi Arabia. Usually, I might not have engaged in any meaningful conversation but I was rebuilding myself. I ended up going skiing with the students and they taught me a life lesson. I always assumed (being ignorant) that Saudi Arabia was all desert with snakes and camels. They taught me some history and shared some pictures. It blew my mind because Saudi Arabia looks like New York City in certain areas but here in the U.S. we do not learn about that information. Experiences like this helped to keep me focused on rebuilding myself and my journey to my purpose.

The night I mentally fought fear during my rebuilding process, I sat down and thought about everything I loved to do in life. Not only did I think about them, but I wrote them down.

I needed to have a plan for my life, set some goals, and more importantly find something I loved doing that could keep my attention. I asked myself, "What have I done in my life that I always enjoyed and could do it for free if I had to?" This was easy because I always enjoyed working with youth. Little did I know, this one question alone would help with the rebuilding process of the new me and open so many doors academically, socially, professionally, and be the start of a new life.

What's so important in the rebuilding process is our ability to be comfortable with not knowing the outcome but having faith that there is something great for us on the other side of this process. Remember, chapter four was about thinking positive and this will be a key ingredient to rebuilding ourselves. The day we lose faith in ourselves and our ability to think positively, this will almost immediately slow down or stop our rebuilding process.

Prepare for a battle with fear. Understand fear is something we all have to deal with but fear is not something we have to give into. One of the best ways to battle fear is to know that it's coming and answer fear by committing to small steps. We don't have to do something great to fight against fear, sometimes it starts with something as small as writing down our goals so we can visually see them every day. This will remind us of the direction we're headed toward while fear tries to tell us otherwise.

Writing my goals down on paper helped me remember what I wanted to accomplish during my rebuilding process and it helped me stay focused on the new me. The old me would not have done anything for my future plans. There is something about writing down your thoughts that makes them more real. Too many of us have thoughts and that is all they are. When we can physically see what we've thought about and place them in places where they constantly remind us of our journey through the rebuilding process, I believe we hold ourselves more accountable than when they are just thoughts in our mind.

So what will you do when the rebuilding process is needed? Are you in the rebuilding process? How many times will you go through this process? We must ask ourselves these questions and begin our new journey filled with purpose and see the potential we have inside. Remember, one source defines the word rebuild as, "to repair, especially to dismantle and reassemble with new parts." Our new parts are waiting for us. Go get them!

Notes

CHAPTER 8
The ISM's of Life

"When you understand ISM'S, you begin to understand the world we live in."

-Unknown

Part of rebuilding ourselves also means understanding other factors in our environment, our lives, and in ourselves that affect how we view the world. We all see the world through a certain lens that is shaped by our experiences. For example, if I was taught growing up that people who did not have college degrees are good for nothing and I watched my family treat people without college degrees differently, it is very likely I would have these same views as an adult. Also, if we were taught, people with different color skin than us are bad and that's all we knew from our childhood, we may treat people who do not have the same skin color as us extremely bad because we don't know any better. This is where the ISM's of life must be understood or at least brought to our attention because there is a direct connection with our "Identity" and our journey toward our purpose.

When I say, "The ISM's of Life" some are probably wondering, "What in the hell are ISM's?" So here is a list of some ISM's you may or may not be familiar with.

Racism	Sexism	Ageism
Ableism	Feminism	Classism
Homophobia (also an ism)	Heterosexism	

Isms are important because of the way they impact our interactions, our opinions of others, our willingness to connect, our reasons to apply for a job, whether or not we will ask for help, and many others. For example, I will never forget the days when I would say things like, "That's gay" or "Look at those faggots." Even now as I write, I feel horrible about the language I used. The language I used was very offensive to populations of people attracted to the same sex. I also remember, around the age of nine or ten, my grandmother asking me to wash the dishes and I said, "Washing dishes is for girls." She immediately put me in my place and made sure I realized men and women can do the same thing. Then I thought about it, my grandmother would always cut the grass in her yard with no problem.

Just imagine becoming lost in our journey toward our purpose because we never realized how one of the ism's caused us to have a one dimensional outlook on certain groups of people. If I would have continued to have sexist beliefs about women and an opportunity within my purpose involved me doing something I thought was only for "Women", I would miss out on many opportunities. Here are a few other specific examples about ism's.

Racism

Merriam-Webster dictionary defines <u>racism</u> as, "a belief that race is the primary determinant of human traits and capacities and that racial differences produce an inherent superiority of a particular race." Although academic scholars and research have their own definition of racism, we will use Merriam-Webster's definition.

We should also acknowledge the differences between "Overt Racism" and "Covert Racism." <u>Overt</u> is defined as, "open and observable; not hidden, concealed, or secret." An example of overt racism would be someone calling a black person a "Nigger" to their face. <u>Covert</u> is defined as, "concealed or secret, not openly practiced, avowed, engaged in, accumulated or shown." An example of covert racism would be an organization speaking all about diversity, making sure their brochures about their organization include pictures of different races and ethnicities, say all the right things when discussing racism, but when it comes down to actions/decisions they continue to make decisions that exclude specific groups of people. Covert racism could also be aligned with Systemic Racism.

Close your eyes and think about the first time you ever encountered racism in your life. You could have been the person who did the racist act or you could have been the one who had the act against them. How did you feel when the encounter happened? How did you react? Did you see this encounter coming before it happened? On a level from 1-10, how intense was this racist interaction? Could you have handled it differently?

I've had several encounters with racism but as

I think about my first one, I do not remember if there were others before. However, when I was in the third or fourth grade, I played basketball. I would say that I was probably the best player on my team and this was my first time playing organized basketball. I was also the only black person on the team. I remember stealing the ball from the other team's point guard over and over again. I was just playing defense. After the third or fourth time stealing the ball from the other team's point guard during the game, my coach who was a white male took me out of the game with this angry look. He told me that I needed to back off or I would not play in that game again.

It's interesting because I remember feeling embarrassed and confused because I thought I was doing my job by playing good defense. I asked my father why that happened and he kind of shook his head. I did not understand at the time but I think that was my first experience with race/racism. Maybe the coach was not being racist but the feeling from that encounter and being the only black male on that team made me feel as though something was not right about that day.

Another way to describe that situation is to call it a "Microagression." A few scholars define Racial Microagression as, "A brief and commonplace daily verbal, behavioral, or environmental indignities, whether intentional or unintentional, that communicate hostile, derogatory, or negative racial slights and insults towards people of color." Those who inflict racial microaggressions are often unaware that they have done anything to harm another person.

Samples of Racial Microaggressions

When speaking to someone of Mexican descent:	Someone asks, "Do you speak Mexican?"
When speaking to someone who is black:	Someone says, "You don't act like the rest of the black people I know."
When speaking to someone of Asian descent:	Someone says, "I know you are smart, all Asians are smart."
When speaking to someone who is not white:	Someone says, "You talk so white."

We are all at different levels in our understanding of "Racism" and as we grow, we will look back at racial situations in our lives and have a better understanding of the experience. ISM's impact us all, especially racism and it's important to gain as much knowledge as we can and implement what we've learned in our lives.

Classism

Merriam-Webster dictionary defines <u>classism</u> as, "prejudice or discrimination based on class." We must acknowledge class because we are all part of a particular social class according to society. We are exposed to different things depending on class. We have access to different resources depending on class. We can be treated differently by others depending on our perceived class. We can also lose ourselves, fighting to be looked at as though you are part of a different class.

There are many misconceptions I had about people who grew up in different neighborhoods than the one I grew up in. I am also pretty sure there are many misconceptions about people from my neighborhood. For example, I used to think that all the people who lived in predominately white neighborhoods were rich and did not have any issues. I thought all the kids who went to school in the suburbs were all smart. This is similar to people believing that all kids from the so called "Hood" or "Ghetto," are gang members and sell drugs. Or, because you did not grow up with your parent(s), you must have had a rough life.

I mention these examples because often we see people and immediately place them in a perceived class based on nothing but physical appearance. Once we place them in a certain social class, we begin to think we know everything about them. Finally, because we think we know everything, we begin to treat them a certain way. This happens too often and it begins to create a sense of "I know what's right" and "My way is the right way."

When we understand being raised in different social classes causes us to think differently than each other, then we may stop and think about the three to five seconds that we take to figure someone out. We can question our immediate thoughts and begin to ask ourselves, "Why do I think this?" and "How could I make a better judgment about this person or group of people?" What social class were I raised in? What social class do people think I was raised in? How do you feel when all of these judgments are made about you and not one of them is true? We must ask ourselves these questions and always remember to understand the effects our social class had on us and others. Classism affects us all and impacts your everyday life!

Ableism

Ablelism is one of the ism's that many of us are not aware of. *Merriam-Webster* dictionary defines ableism as, "discrimination or prejudice against individuals with disabilities." Ableism is not something we often plan to do but because of the world most of us live in, we inherit a certain belief on what it means to be "able." Let me explain.

When a baby is born, the doctor often says, "ten fingers and ten toes." There are certain milestones for babies as they grow older. Milestones like holding their head up on their own, crawling, walking, talking, and many others. I use this example because I know I made many comments about my son being born with ten fingers and ten toes. I also remember having this fear of my son not being physically and mentally developed.

I'm not saying it's bad to want babies to be healthy but what I am saying is, even before babies are physically born, we are filled with thoughts about what it means to be "able." Often, anything less than what is considered the "norm" is looked upon as, "something is wrong." There are even certain places in the world where babies are cast out if they do not have all of their body parts when they are born. Take a second to reflect on this.

Understand, being able has different meanings for different people. Too often ableism clouds our beliefs about others, makes us feel superior to people in the world who do not have the same abilities as us, causes us to pass down false information to our youth about people with disabilities, and lastly we forget about things we have in life that we take advantage of because we believe it's "normal."

We forget our ability to walk and run is a privilege that everyone doesn't have. We forget being able to communicate with our voice is something everyone does not have. We forget seeing and hearing is not something everyone can do. We forget waking up in the morning and brushing our own teeth and washing our own hair is not something everyone can do. We forget being able to think without hearing voices in our head is a privilege.

We forget that our ability to take care of ourselves on a daily basis is a privilege that everyone does not have and sometimes we don't respect it until its gone. We forget!

Ableism affects us all and we don't even know it until we sit down and think about all of the privileges we have that we may call small. We should try our best to respect what we are able to do but more importantly respect others who are not as able but realize they have many abilities as well. We may never totally get rid of ableism, however we should push ourselves to rethink how we view others through the eyes of an able bodied person. Remember, it can all be taken away from you. Respect it!

Heterosexism

Merriam-Webster dictionary defines heterosexism as, "discrimination or prejudice against homosexuals." Homosexual is defined in the *Merriam Webster* dictionary as, "of, relating to, or characterized by a tendency to direct sexual desire toward another of the same sex." To be clear, heterosexuals are attracted to the opposite sex (Male attracted to Female or Female attracted to Male). Homosexuals are attracted to the same sex (Male attracted to Male and Female attracted to Female).

This is a very sensitive topic for many of us to talk about, read about, or even to discuss. It could be because of our religious affiliation, the way we've been taught by society, or just the uncomfortable feeling of discussing something that we are unfamiliar with. We should ask ourselves, "How many times have I had the discussion about Heterosexism in my life?" Next, think about the people who we could have the conversation with. For many of us, there are not a lot of people we could discuss this topic with and have an informed discussion. To get even deeper, we don't even realize the way this topic impacts our everyday interactions.

For a long time I believed the world was full of heterosexuals and whenever I would see something different, I would say things like, "That's gay!" or "Look at those fags!" or "Get that gay shit out of here!" Some of the reasons I was this way is because I was only around heterosexuals (so I thought). All of my friends were attracted to the opposite sex and all of our conversations were about the opposite sex. Church also sent the message that heterosexuality was right and anything else was wrong. Now, I could have misinterpreted the messages I received in church but I am pretty sure I was correct on the interpretation of the church message about heterosexuality. It was not just the church who sent this message but other religious domains seemed to have similar beliefs from my understanding.

I will be honest, it is okay to believe whatever you want in regards to the topic of heterosexism. However, if you believe something because of your religious or spiritual beliefs, it is very important for you to respect and love those who do not believe the same as you. Too often our heterosexist unconscious beliefs make us treat others as though they are less than and we do to others exactly what we don't want happening to us. We do the exact opposite of what our religious or spiritual belief teaches, and we drive people further away from loving human connection.

What decisions have you made over the last year that caused you to lose out on an opportunity because of your heterosexist beliefs? Maybe there were not any but we all accidentally place our heterosexist beliefs above others. Pay attention to how heterosexism plays a role in your life and make sure you learn to control these thoughts.

Sexism

Merriam-Webster dictionary defines sexism as, "prejudice or discrimination based on sex; especially discrimination against women." How often have we heard someone make a sexist comment? How often have you made a sexist comment? What is it about our beliefs of women that causes us to think, feel, and act like they are beneath men? These are questions we must ask ourselves and we need women to help us change the way we view them.

I remember when I would say things like, "A woman shouldn't work at places where heavy lifting is needed." I would say, "I hate going to women's basketball games because they are just not athletic." Having thoughts like this is already harmful but I would actually say these things out loud. I can't imagine what it feels like for a woman to hear men make silly comments about what women can and can't do.

I have to admit, as men, sometimes we don't know any better and our belief system about women and the role of women are completely wrong. For some of us, we look past all the possibilities of a woman and only see women having the ability to give birth, wash dishes, cook dinner, take care of kids, and provide motherly like love. We don't see their ability to practice basketball with a young male, owning their own company, working a physically intensive job, being president of a country, or even becoming a mixed martial arts champion.

Now, I will respect and acknowledge some young men who were raised in a culture where gender roles are set. Women do this and men do that. However, this is the time where we begin to relearn everything we've been taught and take on a new way of thinking. Admit we have inherited society's sexist views without knowing it. Throw out the sexist attitude and commit ourselves to a way of thinking that uplifts women. Think about the ways sexist attitudes affect our mom, sisters, aunts, grandmothers, and all the other women in our lives. The task is not easy and we will say and do things we should not do but remember, it's always a journey when we are training ourselves to think differently than we're used to.

Sexism is alive and well and affects both genders but too often it affects our women in the world more than our men. Take the time to understand what sexism is about and how it finds a way into our lives. As men, sometimes we can't escape it but we must try hard to rid ourselves of many of the negative beliefs and actions toward women.

Ism's play a role in our everyday lives and our journey toward our purpose but many of us never pay close attention to them. We don't have the right to act like ism's are not present. For too long many of us have ignored these ism's and could not figure out why we think the way that we do. It is very important to learn about the ism's that seem most present in our lives and know the ways in which they negatively affect our thoughts and actions. Ism's have the ability to negatively affect us unconsciously and knock us off our journey toward our purpose.

You have been taught how to talk about many of the ism's and what that means is, "You have been taught not to talk about them." Have some conversations with friends and family about any or all of these ism's. These ism's aren't going anywhere but our purpose and identity can elude us if we do not actively engage in learning how ism's impact our lives.

(Secret: Be very careful with who you talk to and learn about ism's. Some people act like they know but they don't. It's not always about what you say, but what you do that counts.)

Notes

CHAPTER 9
Building Your Team

"The strength of the team is each individual member. The strength of each member is the team."

- Phil Jackson

What is it about professional sports teams that always win championships? What is it about companies that always maintain high levels of revenue and respect? What is it that causes entertainers to rise to the top? Let me tell you! It's the same thing we all must have to reach levels that we have never imagined that are aligned with our purpose. A TEAM!

Anybody who is successful at what they do, worked on themselves as an individual but they also made sure they had a team around them to help them move forward. I cannot think of one person who did everything on their own and made it to the top. You get some people who may have inherited a family business but even then, there is some level of team or the business would not be functioning well enough to pass along to family members.

A great example of needing a team is new music artists who are trying to become stars. There is so much work that comes along with being a music artist and there is no way they can do it on their own. Music artists have stylists, accountants, lawyers, security, managers, record labels, choreographers, backup singers, bands, audio engineers, producers, writers, deejay's, and so many more people that help them become a star. Even before artists are at a level where they need accountants and lawyers, they need to get their music out to the world and there is no way to do everything on their own.

Another example could be sports teams. Every team is made up of individuals who have a role on the team. Some roles are more important than others(that's what some say) however, all of the roles are important. Sports teams like the Celtics, Lakers, Bulls, Patriots, Packers, Yankees, and many others, have become well known franchises because they have all mastered the ability to establish great teams at some point. You can never win championships in sports without individuals sacrificing for the team and the team sacrificing for the individuals. When one person becomes too big for the team, often it is the beginning of the end for that franchise.

How often have you taken the time to think about the type of people you need on your team to win championships in the game of life? What type of team do you have right now? How did these teammates get on your team? Do your teammates have what it takes to keep you on the path toward your purpose? Do you have the strength to release players from your team if they are causing you to move in the opposite direction of your purpose?

Questions like these are the questions we should ask ourselves daily, weekly, monthly, and yearly because there should always be an evaluation of ourselves and the people around us. This can be hard because some people have been in our lives for a while and we assume they have a permanent spot on our team. Well let me give you a wakeup call and let you know that friends and family who have been around forever also have the ability to be kicked off the team!

Understand what it takes to maximize our

potential headed toward our purpose. Sports teams change all the time. Some players stay with the same team for their entire career and others play on multiple teams. Our team is the same way! We may have someone who has been around since elementary school. We may also have someone we met a few months ago. Evaluate who is good for our lives and keep them on the team. If they continue to cause trouble, bring negativity, hate on what we want to do, talk about us behind our back, make us feel as though they cannot be trusted, they probably need to be off the team and either kept at a distance or out of our lives as soon as possible. Yes, this is hard when it's close friends or family but sometimes they are the worst people on our team and it is up to us to be realistic about their spot on the team.

I have been lucky to have some great people on my team and they have been in my life for a long time. I hang around the same friends and family from my childhood (Larry House, Marques Ivy, Phil Calvert, Marcus "EMJAY" Johnson, Henry Redd, Donnie Sims). The great thing about my core group of friends and family is that, all of them are doing something positive.

Years of being around this group, I have never had to deal with anyone talking bad about me and they have always pushed me to pursue my purpose. There have been others in my life that were around for short periods of time but my core remains constant because they provide me with what I need. Positivity, personal examples to follow, new knowledge, encouragement, love, and most of all the ability to say I have great people in my life and on my team. We all can't say that but it should always be a goal to have great people in our lives who make up our team. Go back to the question, "Who does your team consist of right now? Are the people on your team aligned with what you want in life?"

I will never forget the day I was in the shower and my mind started to spin because the 4P's continued to come to mind. As I was in the shower I started thinking like I always do and I was trying to figure out why the 4P's continued to come to mind. When I got out of the shower, it finally hit me. Often some of us have the wrong people on our team and we don't understand why we're not progressing the way we should.

There are people who want to be millionaires but they only associate themselves with people who don't have a millionaire mentality. There are people who want to be great athletes but they only associate themselves with people who live the street life. Understanding what it takes to maximize potential and pursue purpose is critical and the 4P's are part of it.

The 4P's

"You are a **PRODUCT** of the **PEOPLE** you **PLACE** in your **PRESENCE**!"

This is all about building our team and making sure people fit. There is no reason for us to be upset about failing out of high school or college when all of the friends around us (OUR TEAM) never went to class. There is no reason for us to be upset about not making the basketball team because we were hanging on the block with (OUR TEAM) and never practiced. There is no reason we should be mad about someone starting their own company with the same idea we were thinking of when we never took the time to build ourselves or (OUR TEAM). When we understand how negative or positive energy within our team can spread to individual members, we then understand how important it is to have a team around us with our best interests in mind. Be mindful because we can't get too selfish and think that everyone should only focus on us. Our team should know, they're always representing us and we respect them enough to know we're always representing them as well.

I always think about romantic relationships when thinking about the 4P's. There have been romantic relationships that involves a man and a woman that have been together for years. The woman says, "I have your back no matter what" to the man. This means, she will be there for her man no matter what happens. When we first hear this comment, it sounds like someone we want on our team. However what we don't realize is that we must hold our teammates accountable the same way we hold ourselves accountable.

The woman in this example has a professional career and is in a relationship with a man who has been in and out of jail/prison because of drug related criminal activity. Now rethink about the woman saying to the man, "I have your back no matter what." Should she have this mentality for the man that is part of her team but is not holding himself accountable for the issues his actions may cause her?

What we should be aware of is the importance of having people on our team that understand they are a direct reflection of us and their decisions can most definitely impact our well being. Think about it, if a drug deal went bad and people came looking for the man in this relationship, the woman would now be in danger. She had nothing to do with the drug deal, but because of a decision "he" made, "she" is now in danger. Since the man who is part of her team was not accountable for the way his actions could affect her (the teammate), everyone is now in danger. Individuals and the team must always think about the impact of both sides because, "We are a Product of the People we Place in our Presence."

Building our team is vital to our journey toward our purpose. The 4P's will help us in all areas of life but we also must be willing to remove people from our team when necessary or keep them at a distance!

YOUR TEAM

What is your ultimate goal?

Name 5-7 people who you consider to be on your team.

1.   5.

2.   6.

3.   7.

4.

What are they doing in their lives?

What is it about these people that cause you to keep them in your life?

What do you contribute to the team?

Who should continue being on your team?

Notes

CHAPTER 10
Don't Get it Twisted!
"No matter where you are from, your dreams are valid."

- Lupita Nyong'o

If you have arrived at this chapter and feel like there is no room in our lives to dream, go back to chapter six and "Check Yourself." When you read the title, "Pursue Your Purpose, Not Your Dreams," that does not translate into, "Do not dream." What I hope for us to do is begin the conversation of **Purpose** vs. **Dreams** with our family and friends and begin to understand the difference between our "Dreams" and our "Purpose."

Let's understand something about dreams. Although dreams are something that may or may not come true, dreams are important because it gives us the ability to create possibilities in our mind and sometimes those possibilities give us the will power to keep moving during times where there may or may not be other options. However, we must be clear that even though these dreams may give us new life, it does not mean they will come true for us. Understanding the way we've been conditioned to chase after dreams that lead us in the opposite direction of our purpose is crucial. Although some of us chase after our dreams and it aligns with our purpose, many of us do not recognize when our dreams are leading us in the wrong direction and that is where the problem with pursuing your dreams comes in.

I recently watched the Oscars (movie awards) and a young lady named Lupita Nyong'o, born in Mexico but raised in Kenya, won best supporting actress for her role in the movie, "12 Years a Slave."

Her acceptance speech was touching because I could see the passion and feel her emotion. As she closed her acceptance speech she said, "No matter where you are from, your dreams are valid." I was so happy for her, I felt like I won the Oscar! As I sat on my couch for a few minutes, I began to process that last line of her speech because she did not say "Dream Big" or "Follow Your Dreams" like so many people in the world tell us, she said "Your Dreams are Valid."

That last phrase, "No matter where you are from, your dreams are valid" has so much depth. It's telling us that dreaming is okay, we have the right to dream whatever we want, and it's also important for us to gain a deeper understanding of what it means when we dream of becoming or doing something. We have a habit of conditioning people with phrases like "Dream Big" or "Follow Your Dreams," and there is nothing wrong with those phrases except they can lead us into false purposes if we do not put those phrases in context. I wanted to make sure you understood my interpretation of the phrase from the Oscar winner because your dreams are truly valid no matter what, especially when you have an understanding of self.

Think about it, what is it about you and your life that makes your road to your purpose more difficult? Is it the negative thought process you may have on life? Is it possibly the people you have around you that makes it hard for you to head toward your purpose? Maybe it's one of the ism's that has trapped you into thinking a certain way or maybe it's something else you may or may not have read in this book. What do you think it is?

Your life is exactly that! YOUR LIFE! Even though we have pressure from so many outside forces, take the challenge with yourself to become a person living in their purpose. Be comfortable with the uncomfortable because as you begin to take steps toward your purpose, you will find yourself frustrated, sad, happy, surprised, excited and most of all fulfilled because there is no better feeling than finding your purpose.

You have read about different areas of life that are important to our individual journeys toward our purpose. Do not think our actions will change overnight. We like to skip right to the action steps when in reality, we must first change the way we think. With new ways of thinking comes new action. Remember this is a process with many different layers. Continue to dream all you want but don't get it twisted and remember to Pursue Your Purpose, Not Your Dreams!

Notes

Joe Johnson "Wise Words"
"Help Seeking"

I remember a student coming to see me toward the end of the college semester about the possibility of him not passing one of his classes. I asked questions like, "What are you struggling with in the class?" and "Have you discussed these issues with your professor?" The student replied with, "I don't talk to my professor, I don't ask for help!" I remember feeling upset with him but I was also very concerned because many of us fall victim to the "I don't ask for help" syndrome and we stay stuck in the circumstances we are trying to relieve ourselves from.

We often may have too much pride to ask for help or our ego overshadows our need to seek guidance. Some of us may be the leader of our family or friends and we feel like we should always know it all. We think asking for help makes us look weak. We also have a hard time figuring out the right question(s) to ask or "how" to ask the right question(s). Unfortunately, some of us then decide not to ask the question at all.

I was always taught to ask questions if I didn't know and to get help when needed. None of us have the ability to navigate this world without help or guidance from others. There are many reasons we don't seek out help but asking for help is a sign of strength and maturity. More importantly, asking for help is always the start to increasing the knowledge we use to guide us in our journey toward our purpose.

While we're in school, we must ask for help. When we have physical and mental health issues, seek out help. When we want to be better in our job or career, seek help. When we are having issues with our relationships, ask for help. When we want to be better at life and live purposefully, we must all "ASK FOR HELP!"

Thank You!

Special Thank You To:
All School Counselors (The Good One's)
Future 4 Teens
Future 4 Teens Participants
Jerusalem Missionary Baptist Church
(Milwaukee, WI)
Praise Temple Church (Milwaukee, WI)
Milwaukee Public Schools (WI)
1998-1999 Bay View High School Basketball
and Football Teams (Milwaukee, WI)
Kalamazoo Public Schools (MI)
Bangor Public Schools (MI)
OAS AIM Students (FL)
Alachua PACE Center for Girls (FL)
Lewis Walker Institute for the Study of Race
and Ethnic Relations
Hispanic American Council (Kalamazoo, MI)
Lake St. Boys & Girls Club (Kalamazoo, MI)
Great Lakes Intercollegiate Athletic Conference
(GLIAC)
Coaching Staff of the Hillside Broncos
(Milwaukee, WI)

Resources

Contact Information:
www.joejohnsonspeaks.com
joejohnsonspeaks@gmail.com
Twitter: @jjohnsonspeaks
Instagram: @joejohnsonspeaks
Facebook: Joe Johnson Speaks

Joe Johnson Speaks
www.joejohnsonspeaks.com

Future 4 Teens
www.future4teens.com

Make sure you Google (Joe Johnson "Wise Words") for Motivation, Inspiration, and Knowledge.

JOE JOHNSON|SPEAKS

Joe Johnson Biography

Joe Johnson was born in Milwaukee, WI but has lived in several places during his childhood including Hawaii and New York. He considers Milwaukee, AKA: "The Mil" his hometown because of the family ties.

Joe Johnson understands the meaning of struggle but has lived with a mentality instilled in him by his mother, "I can do and be anything I want in life." Johnson learned the value of education from both parents but as he began his love for sports at an early age, his focus with competing on the football field and basketball court caused him to develop a "who cares" attitude toward his education.

Growing up in the inner-city of Milwaukee allowed for Johnson to almost fall victim to what many young males were doing in his neighborhood. Sports were his key out of a city where many black and Latino males were often victims of gang violence and self-destruction. After becoming a high school standout football and basketball player, his education finally caught up with him when Division 1 colleges passed on him when finding out his grade point average (1.6) and his score of 13 on the ACT (standardized test). After taking the long route by attending community college then enrolling in a university, he understood education and its affect but he continued his mediocre classroom habits with hopes of playing professional football. Although the opportunity to play professional football was close, his dream faded away and Johnson was stuck graduating with his 2.4 college grade point average and no plans about his future.

Johnson soon learned the power of competing in the classroom, the same way he competed in sports. With his new found attitude and focus, he began to excel academically after being accepted into a Master's program. Johnson began to love learning and realized his purpose was working with the youth and allowing others to be inspired by his voice.

As a proud graduate of Milwaukee Bay View

high school, Johnson holds a Bachelor of Arts degree in Business from Saginaw Valley State University and a Master's degree in Counselor Education from Western Michigan University, Johnson is now in pursuit of a PhD. in Counselor Education at the University of Florida and ready to take on the world!

Made in the USA
Coppell, TX
03 December 2021

66990147R00075